# YOUR KNOWLEDGE HAS

**Bibliographic information published by the German National Library:**

The German National Library lists this publication in the National Bibliography; detailed bibliographic data are available on the Internet at http://dnb.dnb.de .

**Imprint:**

Copyright © 2011 GRIN Verlag
Print and binding: Books on Demand GmbH, Norderstedt Germany
ISBN: 9783668950566

**This book at GRIN:**

https://www.grin.com/document/470122

Serafeim A. Triantafyllou

# Digital Revolution, Digital Economy and E-Commerce Transforming Business and Society. The Transition from the Industrial Revolution to the Digital Revolution

GRIN Verlag

**GRIN - Your knowledge has value**

Since its foundation in 1998, GRIN has specialized in publishing academic texts by students, college teachers and other academics as e-book and printed book. The website www.grin.com is an ideal platform for presenting term papers, final papers, scientific essays, dissertations and specialist books.

**Visit us on the internet:**

http://www.grin.com/

http://www.facebook.com/grincom

http://www.twitter.com/grin_com

# Contents                                                    Pages

# The transition from the industrial revolution to the digital revolution


## Serafeim Triantafyllou

**Abstract** | This study is a scientific research that shows the transition from the industrial revolution to the digital revolution. The continuous flow of information and the rapid development of technology in today's times affect many aspects of our everyday life and in particular the economy, the consumer goods and in general the marketplace. These significant facts lead to the Digital Economy or the New Economy and the Information Society. The effects of the Information Society and the Digital Economy have become visible in Greece, even with a time delay.

The Information Technology revolution happens due to the rapid development of the Internet and the continuous development of Electronic Commerce. Digital economy is creating a unique business culture and establishing a network of economic values critical to the next phase of change in our technological society.

In order this research to contribute on the provision of knowledge, a detailed critical analysis has been followed on the above issues. In today's times the need for specialized executives in Greece is a priority especially in the field of the Information Society and the Digital Economy. The employers want to find personnel with skills in order to take advantage of the new technologies and be profitable (Zoe Georganta and David Warner Hewitt, 2004).

This book is not about networking of technology but the networking of humans through technology. Networking, the art of building alliances, is a critical skill for employees at all levels and in all job roles. The people with their knowledge and creativity can offer a lot to wealth creation and social development. This new age is accompanied by some issues on privacy and security that should be taken into serious consideration.


Terms-Keys – Digital Economy, Information Society, Information Technology (IT), Internet, Electronic Commerce, development

# 1. Digital Economy

## 1.1 Defining the Digital Economy

In our effort to define the Digital Economy we consider important to start our research describing the IT revolution. Information Technology has as a basic tool that is personal computers (PCs). PCs are machines for the storage and processing of information. Information is the effect of the proper processing of the raw data. Raw data is unprocessed computer data. The data could either be entered by a user or generated by the computer itself. Because it has not been processed by the computer, it is considered to be "raw data". The digital information in a computer are stored in binary form and in other words in bits. The binary digit (0 or 1) is the basic information that a computer can understand and describes the fact that all the hardware devices and electronic circuits of the computer can understand two basic electric signals that match to 0 or 1.

As Don Tapscott states about digitization:

*"Knowledge can now be stored in digital form or in 0s and 1s. Unlike the traditional economy where information was physical, communication was only possible through the actual movement of people. In the new economy, information in digital form, facilitated by the digital devices allows the free movement of vast amounts of information in the shortest time possible between people in different parts of the world".*

Information Technology describes the storage process and the transition of information into digital form.

As Nirvikar Singh states:

*"Digital Economy includes potential channels through which information technology (IT) affects economic development."*

(Nirvikar Singh, 2003)

The benefits of Information Technology for developing economies are visible from the 90's. Information Technology can improve efficiency and make developing country firms more competitive. The rapid development of Digital Economy was possible due to the support that many firms provided in terms of business capital and due to the financial markets that were directly connected with the development of Information Technology.

4

## 1.2 The steps of development of Digital Economy

Due to the dynamics of the Internet as a channel of dissemination of information and the use of Internet by firms that main aim was to improve their efficiency and competitiveness, a new economy appeared named "Digital or New Economy".

(Nirvikar Singh, 2003)

In particular, from the late 80's some firms started to express their interest about the use of a new technology named Internet and its contribution to further improvement of efficiency and competitiveness. Some businesses in USA started up new dot-com firms and the focus in the new digital economy that started to appear in the overall economy was towards new ways of development of efficiency and competitiveness. Unfortunately in the first years consumers didn't take notice about the dynamics of the Internet and its use in Electronic Commerce. Internet is an ocean of information and enables the free movement of this huge amount of information in short time between people all over the world.

Nowadays, global businesses aim to take advantage of Information Technology and especially Internet in the field of Electronic Commerce. New businesses start up their activity over the Internet and try to enlarge their profits and their efficiency.

## 1.3 Explaining the importance of Internet

Internet became a research tool in a worldwide communication system. As Don Tapscott states about digitization:

*"Knowledge can now be stored in digital form or in 0s and 1s. Unlike the traditional economy where information was physical, communication was only possible through the actual movement of people. In the new economy, information in digital form, facilitated by the digital devices allows the free movement of vast amounts of information in the shortest time possible between people in different parts of the world".*

The internet is a globally connected network system that uses TCP/IP to transmit data via various types of media. The internet is a network of global exchanges – including private, public, business, academic and government networks – connected by guided, wireless and fiber-optic technologies.

The internet is the most cost-effective communications method in the world, in which the following services are instantly available:
- Email
- Web-enabled audio/video conferencing services
- Online movies and gaming
- Data transfer/file-sharing, often through File Transfer Protocol (FTP)
- Instant messaging
- Internet forums

- Social networking
- Online shopping
- Financial services

(Douglas E. Comer, 2007)


## 1.4 The European Digital Economy


European Digital Economy developed in a different way than the American Digital Economy. European citizens use their mobile phones for texting and posting messages through social media and blogs in the Internet more often than the Americans. However, the percentages of produced products and services through the Internet in Europe tend to be arithmetically lower than those in America. There are also some differences between the former and the later States of European Union in terms of adopting and implementing the new policies that emerge in the Digital Economy. However, the fast growing rhythm of development in the Information Technology and New Technologies of Eastern Europe show that the European Digital Economy will be unified. In particular:

- Almost 87% of the European population use standard telephony services, 78% use mobile telephony services and 61% use Internet services.
- While since October of 2006 19% of American citizens used their mobile phone in order to connect to the Internet, 29% of European citizens used the above services.
- Mobile telephone applications and services through the Internet were used a lot from people in Germany and Italy where we had a 34% of citizens to connect to the Internet through their mobile phones.
- The increase that was achieved to the profits of European Businesses in Telecommunications started to decrease by 10% in 2002, by 4% in 2005 and by 3% in 2006 due to the decrease that appeared in the standard telephony field and due to small increase in bandwidth that time.
- From the European countries, the most electronic transactions took place in United Kingdom in September of 2006 and in particular the 52% of the adult users of Internet did transactions electronically. It is important also to mention that in Germany 48% of Internet users, in France 45% of Internet users and in Italy 14% of Internet users did their transactions electronically.
- From 2002 to 2006, telecommunication services lead to an increase by 4.3% of Gross domestic Product (GDP) in European Union. Information Technology services lead to an increase by 0.2% of Gross domestic Product (GDP) in European Union from 2002 to 2006.
- The percentage of unemployment in Eurozone was 7% in May of 2007 and was the lowest percentage that was observed since 1996 and afterwards.

(Daniel B. Britton & Stephen McGonegal, 2007)

**Annual average of profits from electronic transactions / per user in euro (€)**

|  | 2001 | 2002 | 2003 | 2004 | 2005 | Percentage of increase in 2004-2005 |
|---|---|---|---|---|---|---|
| France | 31.60 | 32.10 | 33.10 | 33.50 | 33.30 | -0.8 |
| Germany | 30.90 | 29.00 | 28.40 | 27.90 | 26.00 | -6.8 |
| Italy | 25.20 | 25.90 | 26.70 | 26.40 | 25.70 | -2.4 |
| Spain | 29.10 | 28.80 | 29.00 | 30.70 | 31.40 | 2.5 |
| United Kingdom | 26.60 | 27.00 | 28.30 | 28.90 | 27.70 | -4.0 |

(Source: IDATE)

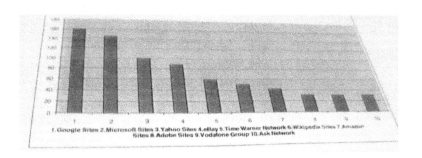

(Source: comScore)

## 1.5 The Chinese Digital Economy

The basic player in the construction sector is China. Furthermore China is a country that invests in Information Technology and Telecommunications in an effort to promote a continuous economic and technological development. In 2006, China had approximately $1 trillion dollars foreign exchange reserves, foreign direct investments of $63 billion dollars and $177 billion dollars trade surplus. The monthly Chinese trade surplus increased at 27% and was $ 26.9 billion dollars in June of 2007. Additionally:

- In 2005 in China were measured 111 million users of the Internet and among them 64.3 million were users of broadband internet connections.
- The Chinese Government introduced some new laws about browsing the World Wide Web in order to ensure bigger security in use of the Internet services.
- Telecommunications are controlled in China from native Chinese firms. China Telecom and China Netcom are responsible for the standard telephony and China Mobile and China Unicom are the basic providers of mobile telephony services.
- In 2006 in China were measured 437 million users of mobile telephony and in particular 301 million of them were subscribed in China Mobile. Comparing the numbers we could say that 301 million users consist the total population of United States of America at that time.

(Daniel B. Britton & Stephen McGonegal, 2007)


### 1.6 The Indian Digital Economy

While China is considered to be the first country where products are produced with low cost, India is considered the best place for supplying companies with low cost services in the Information Technology sector. Additionally:

- In September of 2007, there were measured approximately 60 million users of Internet services and 2.5 million broadband connections
- Also in August of 2007, it was estimated that in India were measured 201 million mobile telephones and 40 million telephone lines
- The Indian industry of the media spent $100 million dollars in 2006 and $300 million dollars in 2010 in Information Technology sector.

(Daniel B. Britton & Stephen McGonegal, 2007)

The most well-known wireless service providers and the subscribed users

|  | September 2005 | March 2006 | June 2006 | September 2006 |
|---|---|---|---|---|
| Wired services | | | | |
| BSNL | 36.8 | 37.5 | 34.9 | 34.0 |
| Wireless services | | | | |
| Reliance | 13.0 | 17.3 | 22.5 | 26.0 |
| Bharti | 14.1 | 19.6 | 23.1 | 27.1 |
| BSNL | 12.4 | 17.7 | 21.0 | 23.7 |
| Hutchison | 9.7 | 15.4 | 17.5 | 20.4 |
| Idea | 5.9 | 7.4 | 8.5 | 10.4 |

(Source: TRAI-Telecom Regulatory Authority of India)


## 1.7 Prevailing trends in profits and the indices of various shares in Information Technology


While technology spending has risen steadily for a decade, the merit of shares of businesses that have invested in new technologies started to rise rapidly. In particular:

- The global marketplace in Informatics and Telecommunications in 2006 was estimated to worth $ 3.15 trillion dollars and $ 1.57 trillion dollars of them had been spent for the development of various form of telecommunications, $ 730 billion dollars had been spent in Information Technology services, $ 537 billion dollars had been spent in hardware and $ 317 billion dollars had been spent in computer software.
- IBM was the biggest Information Technology Company in all over the world in 2006 with sales of $ 48.2 billion dollars. However, the shares of IBM stock in Information Technology sector were only estimated at a 7.2%.

(Daniel B. Britton & Stephen McGonegal, 2007)


## 1.8 The use of information in the production process

Without a doubt, the new technologies changed the structure of the economy. These changes affect the banking sector, the Information Technology sector and generally the Internet.

This type of change is not entirely new. Writing, typography, telegraphy and media inventions (newspapers, radio, television) have had a major impact on the economy, society, have changed the value chains and have led to the creation of new products and services. A value chain is a set of activities that a firm operating in a specific

9

industry performs in order to deliver a valuable product or service for the market (Michael Porter, 1985).

> "The idea of the value chain is based on the process view of organizations, the idea of seeing a manufacturing (or service) organization as a system, made up of subsystems each with inputs, transformation processes and outputs. Inputs, transformation processes, and outputs involve the acquisition and consumption of resources – money, labour, materials, equipment, buildings, land, administration and management. How value chain activities are carried out determines costs and affects profits."

*(IfM, Cambridge)*

Therefore, the question arises as to what is new in the digital economy. The digital economy is the next stage, the stage of the technological innovations of a new era of economic and social change. But can these changes be measured? A more detailed review would lead us to think of parts of the value chain where a new form of information works. The following diagram illustrates the relationship between the customer and the producer of a product that is in demand. It also appears in the diagram that some intermediaries are emerging between the product, the producer and the consumer.

## Illustration of Producer-Product-Consumer Relationship

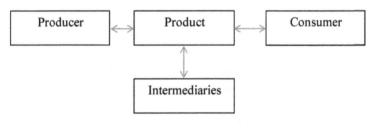

(Source: Beat F. Schmid, 2000)

### 1.9 Digitized Information

Information Technology is based on two basic routes:

1. The officialized and standardized logic

2. The streamlining workflow

In the nineteenth century, after the application of mathematical science to the calculus, we arrived at the beginning of the 20th Century to formalize the processing of information. In the 19th century, the concept of division and segmentation of work, as well as rationalization of the workflow had already been mentioned. In particular, the division of labor was formulated by Taylor and the assembly line by Ford that set the milestones and the main points of the information processing phase (Heinz, 1986).

The calculations based on the analytical geometry provide an official description of space constellations and space-time as well as mathematical physics, as well as industrialization and the nature of the industrial age (Schmid, 1999).

At the present time, we have the next step in formalizing the logic represented by a new science, the science of Information Technology (Schmid, 2000).

## 1.10 The Effects of Digital Economy

The effects of Digital Economy can be depicted in different ways. In our effort to investigate the effects that the Digital Economy exerts, we have to consider how many Internet users use Internet on a daily basis, the number of webpages created, etc.

These measures do not directly measure internet-based economic activity, even though the provision of Internet access is by itself an economic activity. For example, we can name direct transaction data as measures of internet-based economic activity.

Statistics that are often used to measure the growth of Digital Economy are the number of users who access the Internet and the number of websites that are published on the Internet. The US Department of Commerce, using figures from the US Department of Census, reported that 143 million American citizens or 54% of the US population used Internet services in September 2001, while three months earlier, the number of Internet users were 117 million citizens.

On the other hand, the use of the Internet has increased on a global scale. In particular, it was estimated that of 619 million users worldwide, more than half of them used the web services in many languages.

The number of published websites on the internet was estimated to be more than 1 billion websites until January 2000, while in October 1997 it was only 100 million. The number of websites in February 2003 was 36 million sites, while in August 1995 there were 19,000 websites. Over the years, the following figures have emerged: The number of published websites on the Internet has been rising steadily. In particular, in September 2009 it reached 240 million websites, as illustrated by the following chart.

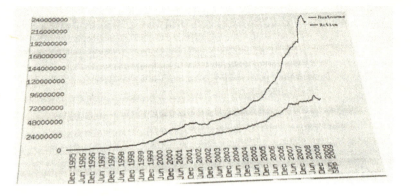

(Nirvikar Singh, 2003) & (http://www.netcraft.com/survey last accessed [21/12/2003])

## 1.11 Management of Organizations in the Digital Economy

Businesses are trying to adapt to the era of Digital Economy, giving emphasis to the creativity and inventiveness of their executives. Consequently management goes through the design, organization and control phase into a phase that gives a particular emphasis on insight, motivation and inspiration (Kostner, 1996).

Moreover in the new era of Digital Economy, the online economy has emerged and the entrepreneurs and the personnel started to give special emphasis to cooperation, inspiration and competitiveness. As illustrated by the following diagram, the key features of Digital Economy are: co-operation, inspiration, authority of competence, knowledge networking, concurrent processes, horizontal communication, trust and integrity. From the other side, the key features of the industrial era were: chain of command, command and control, authority of position, sequential processes, vertical communication and compliance.

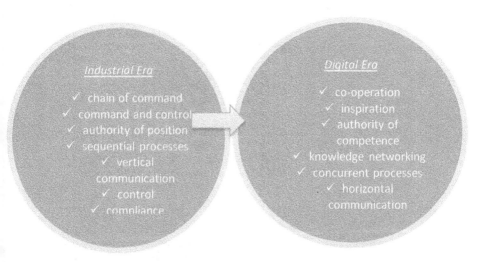

Diagram of the key features of the Industrial era and the Digital era

## 2. Differences between the Traditional and New Economy

The most important difference between the Traditional and New Economy is the transaction cost, that is the basic cost associated with digital products. The transaction cost is constantly decreasing and thus benefits can be gained, such as the ability to make distance transactions 24 hours a day, 7 days a week, 365 days a year. Another difference between the new economy and the traditional economy is the different infrastructure, with more logistics problems to appear in the supply chain management. In particular, there may have been some investments in Greece regarding the management of the warehouse of an enterprise, but from that point until the establishment of an enterprise dedicated to supply chain management, and in particular to the logistics sector, are needed much more to be done. Moreover, in the Digital Economy, we have a new type of consumer who, for the first time, has the tools of searching and choosing the transactions he wants to make (Sarianidis & Kliani, 2008).

## 2.1 The current Greek reality

There was an increase at 62% in the volume of digital data in 2009 worldwide. According to the so-called research "The Digital Universe Decade - Are You Ready?" of IDC the volume of digital data has increased at 62% compared to 2008, reaching 800 billion Gigabytes of data. This specific scientific research aimed to investigate and record the digital data produced annually, as well as their impact on Internet users and professionals in Information Technology. The volume of digital data was estimated to increase to 1.2 trillion in 2019 and would be equivalent to:

- 75 billion full-load Apple iPads of 16 Gigabytes, which could fill 41 times the Wembley stage.
- 707 trillion copies of the new US Health Bill, signed in March 2010, containing 2000 pages. These copies, sequentially placed one behind the other, could cover 16 times the distance from the Earth to Pluto.

According to IDC, the growth rate of digital data volume in the future will be impressive because:

- The volume of digital data produced annually will be increased exponentially 44 times over the period from 2009 to 2020, as all basic media of communication will have been fully transferred from analog to digital form.
- IDC estimates that the increase in funds to be invested in Information Technology and Innovation could generate new revenues for businesses exceeding $ 1 trillion for the period from 2009 to 2014.
- By 2020, the percentage of digital data encrypted will increase from 30% to 50%.
- The volume of digital data produced annually exceeds 35% of the total capacity of the storage devices. This percentage will upcome to 60% the coming years.
- More than 70% of the volume of digital data is generated by Internet users. However, businesses have so far been responsible for protecting, storing and managing 80% of the volume of digital data produced. It has been observed that the volume of digital data has grown exponentially when web 2.0 technologies and especially social media have been utilized by businesses.

(Mallas, D., 2010)

Broadband penetration in Greece stood at 18.6% at the end of the first half of 2010, according to the Information Society Observatory, which noted that it is the highest rate of broadband growth observed in Greece.

The Observatory's report reported an increase in domestic demand compared to the previous half, despite a relative decline in the second quarter of 2010 due to the economic crisis.

Moreover, the cost of broadband connections in Greece relatively to other European states is particularly competitive. There is also an increase in the number of the subscribers using mobile telephone cards and internet services.

The total size of fixed broadband connections amounted to 2,105,076 at the end of the first half of 2010, up 20.1% year-on-year and up 9.8% from the previous half year.

In 2010, the overwhelming majority of broadband lines (2,096,715) were of DSL technology. There were also 8,361 broadband connections of other technologies (leased lines, fiber optic lines, etc.). Greece in 2010 ranked 23rd among the 27 member states of the European Union in terms of broadband penetration, but between 1/1/2009 and 1/1/2010 the increase in broadband penetration in Greece was almost double relatively to the European average.

Greece is at a good level in the speed of broadband connections. In the high-speed package (10 Mbps and above), Greece is among the first EU member states that have fast broadband connections.

Broadband connections coverage at national level increased from 88% to 91%, in urban areas it remained at 100% and in rural areas increased from 55% to 60%, exceeding the rate of increase of the European average (increase of 92.7% to 94% in broadband connections for urban areas and from 76.6% to 80% for rural areas).

The Information Society Observatory estimated that the negative economic conjuncture had not affected the broadband market in the first quarter of 2010, but that eventually occurred in the second quarter of 2010 when the number of new broadband connections had dropped considerably.

In the third quarter of 2010, according to the report, there were no estimates that the overall situation would improve, while estimates at the end of the second half of 2010 would range from 19.6% to 20.2%.

(The Global Information Technology Report 2009–2010 ICT for Sustainability, 2010)

In our effort to come to some conclusions, we would say that:

Triple is the number of internet subscribers worldwide compared to the number of internet subscribers eight years ago. The latest official data reported about 1.46 billion internet-connected residents and internet penetration worldwide in the 21.9% daily. What is worth noting, however, is that according to the latest statistics, China has a greater number of Internet subscribers compared to North America, as we have 253 million citizens connected to the Internet in China while we have 248 million citizens connected to the Internet in North America.

In Europe, Sweden is one of the first places in the Internet penetration rate of 77.4%. Greece, on the basis of the above, is at 18.6% as regards the penetration of broadband in the first half of 2010, as noted by the Information Society Observatory. Specifically, the Information Society Observatory notes that in 2010 there was a high rate of increase in the penetration of broadband in Greece compared to the European average.

("ebusiness forum", 2010)

15

## 2.2 Comparison of the New Economy with the Current Economy

Taking into account that the New Economy is the one that followed after industrial development and traditional industrialization, it is then realized that the New Economy is an anticipated development of capitalism. The evolving economy, is enriched with new prospects and opportunities that lead to more effective satisfaction of needs, reducement of the cost of production and change of the production functions due to the increase in productivity. In the agricultural economy, the main factor of production was the land. Traditional industrialization set the rules of manual labor and mentioned the need of existence of money as key factors of production. On the other hand, in the digital or new economy times, digital economy focuses on the human mind, which is the key factor for evolution and development.

Before the technological revolution was the industrial revolution that dates back to 1780-1840, the Second Industrial Revolution that dates back to 1840 -1890 and the Third Industrial Revolution that dates back to 1890 until 1950. In the Second Industrial Revolution there was development of the railways. The Third Industrial Revolution brought the use of electricity and the development of the automobile industry. By trying to compare the technological revolution of today's era and the previous forms of industrial revolution, we conclude on the following conclusions:

- The technological revolution of today's era is not industrial but intangible and depends to a large extent on profitable and continuous financing.

- The present technological revolution is the first technological revolution whose consequences affect all three key areas of the economy (primary sector, secondary sector and tertiary sector).

- Due to the rapid access to digital information, the New Economy is more transparent in relation to the current traditional economy, allowing price comparisons of similar products and services and preference for the most advantageous price by the consumer. In addition, the New Economy achieves programming of the quantity of products and services produced and the avoidance of the accumulation of significant stocks, because the knowledge of the level of demand for products and services minimizes cost, thus facilitating the optimal allocation of resources and production factors.

- Another important difference between the current technological revolution and the past technological breakthroughs is the need the classical entrepreneur to come up with modern ideas so that he can optimally combine production factors and dare to take risks in entrepreneurship.

- The New Economy goal is not to displace the traditional economy but, on the contrary, the main objective is the harmonious coexistence between them. Moreover, the traditional economy is the basis for the development of the new economy. The new economy enriches the traditional economy by making it more efficient.

16

One question that needs to be answered is whether the digital economy is an actual or an unrealistic economy. The digital economy is indeed a realistic economy and was represented in 2010 by 270 listed firms in global finance markets. The capitalization value of these companies is successively high. In particular, three years ago, the capitalization value of these firms referred to be $ 50 billion, although it was estimated to be increased to $ 1.5 trillion in the coming years (Sarianidis & Kliani, 2008).

**2.3 The thorny sides of the New Economy**

The new economy has several thorny issues that need to be clarified. Particularly:

- With the emergence of new technologies, rumors have been spread about the elimination of economic laws, the failure to link development and inflation rates, and the no risk separation of a real monetary economy and a self-regulating market.
- The shrinking of many businesses is not only the result of new technologies, but we should see why some businesses have not been able to enter the new digital age and grow. However, we can not in any way come to the conclusion that the contraction of some businesses is associated with the changes brought by the New Economy. What has forced many businesses to end their operations is not the intensification of competition but the increase in the monopoly. Also, due to globalization, many businesses are called upon to compete in a global market and this leads small and medium-sized businesses not being able to compete with multinational companies.
- There have been some losses of the internet and the collapse of the new economy as shown by the following tables:

**Table 1: Significant online losses**

| Firms | Price | Annual Change |
|---|---|---|
| Intel World | 3.19 | -96.3% |
| Luminant Worldwide | 1.88 | -95.9% |
| Ventro | 5.69 | -94.9% |
| Calico Commerce | 2.88 | -94.6% |
| IXL Enterprises | 3.19 | -94.3% |
| Open Market | 2.63 | -94.2% |
| Preview Systems | 3.94 | -93.9% |
| NBC Internet | 4.94 | -93.6% |
| Juno On-Line | 2.31 | -93.5% |
| Stamps.com | 2.72 | -93.5% |
| US internet working | 3.09 | -93.4% |
| Internet Capital | 11.63 | -93.2% |
| National Info | 2.50 | -92.2% |
| Consort | 6.19 | -91.5% |
| Allaire | 5.06 | -91.4% |

| Intertrust Tech | 3.81 | -91.3% |
|---|---|---|
| Sykes Enterprises | 3.22 | -91.2% |
| Breakaway Solutions | 2.63 | -90.9% |
| Xpedior | 4.41 | -90.7% |
| Razorfish | 2.94 | -90.7% |
| MP3.com | 34.06 | -90.0% |
| S1Corp | 7.81 | -90.0% |
| Red Hat | 11.31 | -89.3% |
| QRS Corp | 11.38 | -89.2% |
| Priceline.com | 5.19 | -89.1% |
| Viant | 5.50 | -88.9% |
| TenFold | 4.63 | -88.4% |
| Marimba | 5.47 | -88.1% |
| StarMedia Network | 5.06 | -87.4% |
| Scient | 12.19 | -85.9% |

(Source: Financial Times)

**Table 2: The collapse of the New Economy in specific sectors**

|  | 2003 | 2005 |
|---|---|---|
| Energy | 4% | 28% |
| Telecommunications | 6% | 10% |
| Technology | 42% | 22% |
| Finance | 12% | 22% |
| Health | 14% | 8% |

(Source: Business Week)

## 2.4 Risks that lie behind the Digital Economy

The increasing use of the Internet, particularly for downloading digital information and the conduct of financial transactions, is accompanied by a series of risks regarding the users' personal data. Threats, such as spam emails and spyware, have been created to generate a series of new threats such as phishing emails and keylogger software or hardware. Phishing emails and keyloggers are most often used for the purpose of stealing passwords and other confidential information. Moreover, viruses and worms are transmitted through the internet, while spam emails through the email server technology. In general, all these threats are named as malicious software. Malicious software (malware) is any software intentionally designed to cause damage to a computer, server, client, or computer network ("Defining Malware", 2009). The concern to ensure greater Internet safety does not mean minimizing the corporate or personal use of Internet services. A 2006 survey has shown that 91% of businesses consider viruses and malicious software as serious threats and 86% of businesses consider spam emails as possible threat. About 72% of businesses consider the stealing of confidential data as a very serious threat and 25% of businesses have implemented data encryption to secure confidential data from threats. Also, most Internet users besides the fact that are aware of cookies, only 28% of them take seriously the matter of cybersecurity and delete cookies from their computer. One strategy for protecting against malware is to prevent the malware software from gaining access to the target computer. For this reason, antivirus software, firewalls and other strategies are used to help protect against the introduction of malware, in addition to checking for the presence of malware and malicious activity and recovering from attacks ("Protect Your Computer from Malware", 2010).

It is a fact that internet threats are increasing and the need for internet safety is crucial for a safer Internet. According to PC World, in 2006 the five first threats on the Internet were: (1) hackers that send phishing emails, (2) malicious software (3) spam emails, (4) worms on the MySpace.com website etc. Hackers are constantly developing new tactics in their online attacks with main purpose of stealing confidential data. Hackers use keyloggers, trojan horses and other malicious software.

Microsoft takes cybersecurity seriously and implements security operations. In particular, over 3,500 dedicated Microsoft cybersecurity professionals help protect, detect, and respond to threats ("Microsoft").

According to Canalys survey, organizations have increased their level of protection against malicious threats, while respecting the strengthening of compliance regulations for data protection. Computer viruses are now airborne, infecting smartphones and mobile devices in every part of the globe. Security companies, cellular operators and phone makers are moving to quash these threats before they spiral out of control (**Mikko Hypponen,** 2006).

Cost of security seems to be measured by summing up the expenses for the acquisition, deployment, and maintenance of security technology (**Bohme,** 2010). Cybersecurity professionals of many IT firms will protect, detect, and respond to the emergence of new threats.

Additionally it is very important to mention that malicious software is developped and replicated on peer-to-peer (P2P) networks. Symantec estimates that the malicious software will continue to grow and measures should be taken to prohibit its transmission through P2P networks. In particular, 47% of malicious software was transmitted in P2P networks in the last six months of 2006.

(Daniel B. Britton & Stephen McGonegal, 2007)


**2.5 Malicious Software (Malware)**

In the Internet there are many types of threats named as malicious software (malware). In particular, viruses, worms, Trojan horses and spyware are some examples of threats over the Internet.

A computer virus is a type of malicious code or program written to alter the way a computer operates and is designed to spread from one computer to another. A virus operates by inserting or attaching itself to a legitimate program or document that supports macros in order to execute its code. In the process, a virus has the potential to cause unexpected or damaging effects, such as harming the system software by corrupting or destroying data.

A computer worm is a type of malware that spreads copies of itself from computer to computer. A worm can replicate itself without any human interaction, and it does not need to attach itself to a software program in order to cause damage.

Spyware is software that "spies" on a computer. Spyware can capture information like Web browsing habits, e-mail messages, usernames and passwords, and credit card information. If left unchecked, the software can transmit this data to another person's computer over the Internet.

A Trojan horse is a type of malware that is often disguised as legitimate software. Trojans can be employed by cyber-thieves and hackers trying to gain access to users' systems. Users are typically tricked by some form of social engineering into loading and executing Trojans on their systems. Once activated, Trojans can enable cyber-criminals to spy on you, steal your sensitive data, and gain backdoor access to your system. These actions can include:

- Deleting data
- Blocking data
- Modifying data
- Copying data
- Disrupting the performance of computers or computer networks

Unlike computer viruses and worms, Trojans are not able to self-replicate.

Worms account for 52% of Internet threats, and trojan horses from 23% earlier, now account for 45% of Internet threats, according to a survey conducted in 2006.

In 2006 it was noted by specialists that about 1 in 120 emails contained virus. At the end of 2006, a study by Infonetics Research found that viruses were the main reason that companies tried to shield themselves against them. It was also noticed that 80% of malicious attacks over the Internet occurred on marketing sites.

(Daniel B. Britton & Stephen McGonegal, 2007)

Diagram of Malware attacks on computers

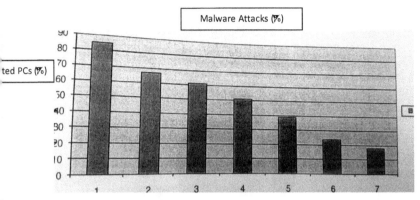

(Source: Webroot Software)

## Table 2: Malware attacks globally

|    |                | Malware attacks (%) |
|----|----------------|---------------------|
| 1  | USA            | 31%                 |
| 2  | China          | 10%                 |
| 3  | Germany        | 7%                  |
| 4  | France         | 4%                  |
| 5  | United Kingdom | 4%                  |
| 6  | South Korea    | 4%                  |
| 7  | Canada         | 3%                  |
| 8  | Spain          | 3%                  |
| 9  | Taiwan         | 3%                  |
| 10 | Italy          | 3%                  |

(Source: Symantec)

The continuing increase in spam emailing creates problems. Symantec estimates 54% of spam emails in the first half of 2006 and 59% of spam emails in the second half of 2006. It is also estimated that 0.68% of spam emails contains malicious software (malware).

(Daniel B. Britton & Stephen McGonegal, 2007)

## Spam categories for the second half of 2006

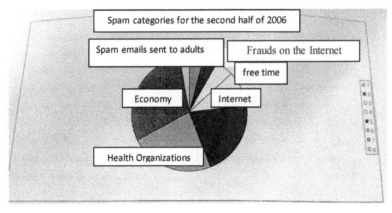

(Source: Symantec)

## Spam Emailing across many countries (%)

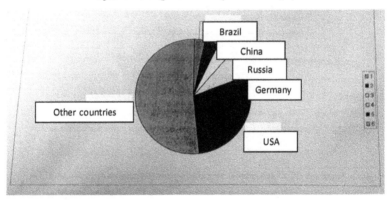

(Source: Comm Touch)

### 2.6 Phishing

Phishing is the fraudulent attempt to obtain sensitive information such as usernames, passwords and credit card details by disguising as a trustworthy entity in an electronic communication. Typically carried out by email spoofing or instant messaging, it often directs users to enter personal information at a fake website, the look and feel of which are identical to the legitimate site.

22

Vishing is the telephone version of phishing, or a voice scam, designed to trick victims into sharing personal information, such as PIN numbers, social security numbers, credit card security codes, passwords and other personal data.

Spear phishing is an email or electronic communications scam targeted towards a specific individual, organization or business. Although often intended to steal data for malicious purposes, cybercriminals may also intend to install malware on a targeted user's computer.

Pharming is another scam where a fraudster installs malicious code on a personal computer or server. This code then redirects any clicks you make on a website to another fraudulent Website without your consent or knowledge.

A Gartner survey showed that in 109 million American adult citizens had been sent phishing emails in 2006, compared to 2004, where was estimated that in 57 million Americans had been sent phishing emails.

A Symantec survey showed that 166,248 phishing emails were sent in the second half of 2006, and this illustrates a 6% increase in more phishing emails between the first and the second half of 2006.

Education is fundamental to every cybersecurity strategy. Industry verticals face unique cybersecurity challenges in their effort to protect organizations, providers and customers.

In cybersecurity a very important responsibility is to ensure data availability, integrity, authentication and confidentiality. A cybersecurity specialist implements and monitors security measures for communication systems, networks, and provides advice that systems adhere to established security standards.

Cybersecurity specialists argued that 95.2% of phishing attacks happened to websites with eshop in June of 2007, 0.7% of phishing attacks happened to the operation of Internet service providers, 1.4% of phishing attacks happened to retail websites and 2.7% of phishing attacks happened to other web sites.

The U.S. Federal Trade Commission reported 221,000 internet-related fraud complaints in 2007. That's 16,000 more than in 2006. It is projected that there will be 260,000 complaints in 2008.

The global economic impact of security fraud is estimated to be between $7 billion and $10 billion annually. As you can imagine, companies that combat fraud and scams are doing very well."Phishing" is the fastest growing and most profitable type of internet fraud. "Phishers" use social-networking schemes to lead consumers to counterfeit websites. They fool the recipients into divulging financial data.

("seekingalpha.com", 2007)

Basically the "Phishers" masquerade as a brand like Paypal, eBay or Bank of America. They send an email that looks very official and ask the reader to verify some personal information. Sometimes, they even threaten to suspend their account if they don't provide the info.

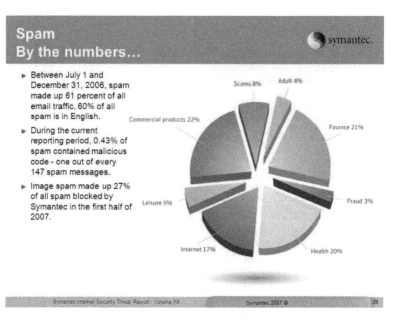

(Source: Symantec)

(Source: Anti-Phishing Working Group)

Google's chart shows that it detects about 300,000 phishing sites per month.

Google prides itself on being proactive in protecting its users from malware and other attacks (even government-sponsored ones) on the Web via its Safe Browsing API and other technologies over the past five years. In a blog post, the company reveals the numbers behind some of its anti-malware initiatives:

Google finds about 9,500 new malicious Web sites per day, either innocent ones that have been compromised by hackers or sites built specifically to distribute malware or for phishing.

About 600 million users of Chrome, Firefox, and Safari see several million warnings per day about malware and phishing on sites the users are about to visit.

About 12 million to 14 million Google Search queries per day display the warning that sites are compromised.

Google provides malware warnings for about 300,000 downloads per day through its download protection service for Chrome.

Google sends thousands of notices to Webmasters daily about malware they need to remove or protect users from.

Phishing pages are often removed within an hour of their detection.

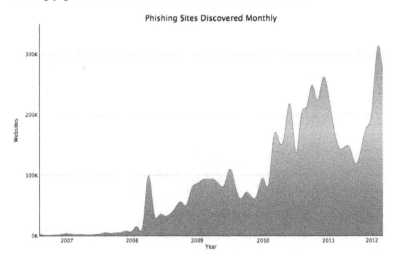

**Phishing Sites Discovered Monthly**

("cnet.com")

25

## 2.7 Indentity theft

Identity theft, also known as identity fraud, is a crime in which an imposter obtains key pieces of personally identifiable information in order to impersonate someone else.

The information can be used to obtain credit, merchandise and services in the name of the victim, or to provide the thief with false credentials.

Identity theft is categorized two ways: true name and account takeover.

True-name identity theft means the thief uses personal information to open new accounts. The thief might open a new credit card account, establish cellular phone service or open a new checking account in order to obtain blank checks.

Account-takeover identity theft means the imposter uses personal information to gain access to the person's existing accounts. Typically, the thief will change the mailing address on an account and run up a huge bill before the person whose identity has been stolen realizes there is a problem. The internet has made it easier for an identity thief to use the information they've stolen, because transactions can be made without any personal interaction.

("TechTarget's IT encyclopedia")

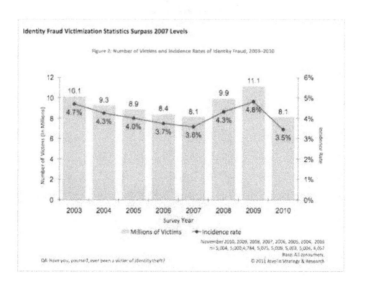

26

While the estimated number of identity fraud victims fell steeply last year from the year prior, consumers' out-of-pocket identity fraud costs rose, according to a report from Javelin Strategy & Research.

According to the 2011 Identity Fraud Survey Report, 8.1 million adults in the United States were identity fraud victims last year, down 28 percent, or three million, from 2009, the largest single-year decrease since Javelin started tracking the data in 2003.

At the same time, however, the average consumer out-of-pocket cost due to identity fraud increased to $631 per incident in 2010, up 63 percent from $387 in 2009. Such costs include the expenses of paying off fraudulent debt as well as resolution fees, such as legal costs.

According to James Van Dyke, president and founder of Javelin Strategy & Research, the decrease in the number of identity fraud victims, and the total amount of annual fraud, can be attributed to efforts of businesses, the financial services industry and the government to educate consumers and prevent and resolve such fraud. Consumers are monitoring their accounts more carefully too, he said. He also cited increased security measures, law enforcement successes and the improving economy as reasons for the decreases.

(Saranow Schultz, J. The Rising Cost of Identity Theft for Consumers

based on Javelin Strategy and Research)


## 2.8 Pirated Software

There are number of methods for obtaining and using counterfeit software. The commonly used ones are obtaining and using counterfeit product keys, obtaining "key generator" programs and using them to create product keys, and obtaining "crack" tools and using them to bypass licensing and activation mechanisms. The results of an investigation by IDC into the prevalence of malicious code and unwanted software at Web sites that offer pirated software, counterfeit product keys, crack tools, and key generators for Microsoft Windows XP and Microsoft Office showed that 25 of the 98 Web sites (25%) hosted malicious or potentially unwanted software; at two-thirds of those were found multiple instances of such software.

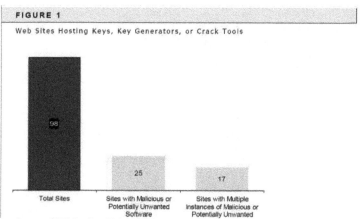

Source: IDC Study, *Risks of Obtaining and Using Pirated Software, 2006*

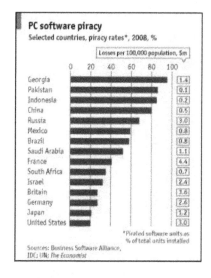

The share of software on personal computers that is pirated rose to 41% last year, according to a report by the Business Software Alliance, a trade group, and ICD, a market-research firm. A further 44% is paid for. The rest is free or open-source. Piracy rates are falling in half of all countries and stable in another third. But in countries where sales of PCs are growing fastest, the piracy rate is high. The worst offender is Georgia, where 95% of all software is unlicensed. The rate is lowest in America but even there, as much as a fifth of software is pirated. In rich western

Europe, around a third of all software is unlicensed. In the big emerging markets, such as China, India and Russia, software piracy has dropped sharply in recent years.

(Source: Business Software Alliance)

It emerges from a recent survey in 110 countries, published by the BSA3 (2009), that 41 % of the installed software, on personal computers is a pirated version, 15 % of freeware and 44 % of compiled software (Heger, 2009).

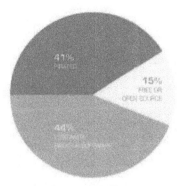

Source: Sixth Annual BSA-IDC Global Software Piracy Study, may 2009

## 2.9 Description of the economic environment

|  | Traditional Economy | New Economy |
|---|---|---|
| Structure | Stability | Flexibility |
| Components | Data, Information | Knowledge |
| Development | Predictability | Information Technology |
| Infrastructure | Traditional | Digital |
| Geographical coverage | Regional | Universal |
| Time constraints | Standard hours | 24 hours a day |
| Products/Services | mass production | Personalized transactions |
| Access points | Central distribution points | Distributed central points including electronic devices |

(Source: "Business Week", 2005)

|  | Administration | Knowledge management |
|---|---|---|
| Structure | Hierarchical | Flexible |
| Development | Predictable | Adapted |
| Integration | Adoption of new technology to upgrade the product | HR & Career Solutions, e-government |
| Capital | Capital, raw materials, manpower, technology | Knowledgebase, raw materials, manpower, technology |

(Source: "Business Week", 2005)

## 3. Some first conclusions about the new or digital economy

The basis of the new economy is the economic and social potential of the relations of in-house consolidations of ideas and novelties. Knowledge and intellectual property are enhanced by the power of the information technology on the globalized economy.

Assuming that an enterprise wishes to follow the aspects and rules introduced by the new economy, then the investment segment of the particular business should be divided into the following two branches:

  a) financial investment analysis and
  b) administrative investment analysis that generates private information.

Financial investment analysis includes scattered information about the current economy, but this information is not part of the businesses. The information is disseminated to customers, suppliers, shareholders, creditors, trade unions, etc. All these things are not part of the traditional economy.

Administrative investment analysis is a component of the New Economy and recommends that those in charge of developing new investments and other economic regulators have to strive to make the innovation of knowledge known financially.

The problem is that investment analysis in its present form is not only possible to assess but also to predict the form of investment.

(Basileiadis, 2007)

Digital Economy is much more than just a simple electronic transaction. The transition to the Digital Economy is a fundamental transition that has been taking place for more than two decades and is based on the decline of cost of processing, storing and transmitting information in digital electronic form.

The transition was made by dot.com businesses that focused their interest in using the internet as a retail and marketing channel. Using the internet as a retail and marketing channel is just one piece of the digital or new economy.

Internal business organization is changing, and the ways of measuring the impact of the digital economy vary. However, according to academic research findings, the continuing impact of the digital economy in the present era is obvious.

(Nirvikar Singh, 2003)


## 3.1 What is required for the Digital or New Economy

Data is required in the New Economy. We also need to measure the information and software infrastructure that exists in the traditional economy and, in particular, measure investment in hardware (such as computers, telephone lines, fiber optics, cable equipment, wireless networks, etc.), to measure investment in software infrastructure, to measure Internet possibilities and telecommunication protocols and in the end to measure the traffic across the computer networks.

(Haltiwanger J. & Ron S. Jarmin)

In the new era of the Internet and the Digital Economy, new rules have been set up in the way of product and service production as well as the need for further education and acquisition of new digital skills to determine the type of data collected by the federal statistical offices and other institutions.

There is a series of unresolved conceptual questions that are in close relation to the measuring of the impact of the economy. For example, it is worth measuring how Information Technology is closely linked to the development of economic sectors.

The emerging digital economy requires statistical services to reconsider how they measure the basic structural elements of outflows, inflows and inflation.

There are some ideas that can be taken into consideration by statistical services in the measurement of data. Specifically:

Digital data-capturing techniques should complement the operation of key measurement software of a country's statistical services, in particular in measuring inputs, outputs and data relating to the basic household economy. Particular emphasis should be placed on improving measurement in those areas of measurement where difficulties are encountered and Information Technology can make a significant contribution to this project.

However, it is worth highlighting that the various changes to the basic data collection software by the statistical services are a long-term process.

(Haltiwanger J. & Ron S. Jarmin)


## 3.2 The New Economy is a Knowledge Economy

Information Technology fosters an economy based on knowledge. However, despite the emergence of artificial intelligence and empirical systems, knowledge has been created and continues to grow by the person seeking knowledge.

"Assisted intelligence and service technology are releasing new forms not only in the tertiary sector but also in the secondary or so-called industrial sector," said James Brian Quinn, a professor at Dartmouth's Tuck School, in the book "The Smart Business".

The Knowledge Economy is significantly developed with the harmonic mixture of consumers' ideas, data and Information Technology.

(Basileiadis, 2007)

*"In today's global economy, companies that claim their leadership position on the market, if they do not follow the digital and technological evolvement, soon will be unable to follow the new marketplace rules."*

said Frank Schrontz, chairman and chief executive officer of Boeing, after the design of Boeing 777 aircraft.

Frank Schrontz also states that:

*"If the world is changing continuously, and we we want to follow the new digital and technological evolution, we must understand our customer needs and try to raise our production line and efficiency by delivering better products and services."*

The information is so fast that Boeing has to harmonize its operation with the new technological developments in order to maintain its strong brand name and reputation and pass from the past to the future.

(Basileiadis, 2007)

## 3.3 The New Economy is a global Economy

MIT Professor Paul Krugman says that the global economy is closely connected with the exchange of products, services, capital, labor and information. Peter Drucker also states that "knowledge knows no borders."

(Basileiadis, 2007)

## 3.4 What is the future of the New Economy?

The slowdown that may take place at some point in the technology sector is not just a guess. An important issue to be discussed is whether the decline in growth will reduce or leave productivity unchanged. Productivity will depend primarily on the growth rate of the economy, secondarily on the pace of growth in the technology sector and thereafter on the pace of investment in the capital goods sector.

In a period of economic recession there is also a drop in productivity. The economic crisis in the United States, which was extended to Europe, was a crash test for the stability of the new economy. The new economy to withstand must have solid foundations in the traditional economy.

(Sarianidis & Kliani, 2008)


## 3.5 Some last conclusions about the Digital Economy

So what are the innovations introduced by the new or digital economy? Innovations are the new technological vehicle of the Internet and the new level of connectivity between heterogeneous ideas and roles which drives the development of a broad range of perspectives and potentials.

The combination of digitization and the Internet enables the collection, processing and distribution of information quickly and efficiently.

The digital economy or the new economy is not a static but a dynamic economy that is inextricably linked to new products and new activities by making implementation of innovative ideas through the use of Information Technology.

(Bo Carlsson, 2004)

## 4. The basic features of Electronic Commerce (eCommerce)

The management guru Peter Drucker said about Electronic Commerce:

> *"The truly revolutionary impact of the Internet Revolution is just beginning to be felt. But it is not "information" that fuels this impact. It is not "artificial intelligence." It is not the effect of computers and data processing on decision making, policymaking, or strategy. It is something that practically no one foresaw or, indeed even talked about 10 or 15 years ago; e-commerce- that is, the explosive emergence of the Internet as a major, perhaps eventually the major, worldwide distribution channel for goods, for services, and, surprisingly, for managerial and professional jobs. This is profoundly changing economics, markets and industry structure, products and services and their flow; consumer segmentation, consumer values and consumer behavior; jobs and labor markets. But the impact may be*

*even greater on societies and politics, and above all, on the way we see the world and ourselves in it." (Drucker, 2002, pp. 3-4)*

Electronic commerce or e-commerce is a business model that lets firms and individuals conduct business over electronic networks. In particular, Electronic commerce is a business model in which transactions take place over electronic networks, mostly the Internet. It includes the process of electronically buying and selling goods, services, and information (**Turban, King, Lee,Liang and Turban (n.d.)**). Electronic commerce operates in all four of the following major market segments:

- Business to business (B2B)
- Business to consumer (B2C)
- Consumer to business (C2B)
- Consumer to consumer (C2C)

Electronic commerce is one of the main criteria of revolution of Information Technology in the field of economy. Certainly can be claimed that electronic commerce is canceled many of the limitations of traditional business. The form of traditional business has fundamentally changed and these changes are the background for any decision taken in the economy. Existence of virtual markets, virtual stores(e-shops) that have not occupy any physical space, allowing access and circulation in these markets 24 hours a day from anywhere in the world is possible. Select and order goods that are placed in e-shops or virtual stores and e-commerce transactions that are conducted through virtual networks where payment is provided through electronic services, all of these options show that electronic commerce is a digital revolution of our century. E-commerce, which can be conducted over computers and mobile devices (smartphones, tablets) may be thought of as a modernized version of mail-order catalog shopping. Nearly every product or service is available through e-commerce transactions, including books, music, plane tickets, and financial services such as online banking services (Bloomenthal).

Interaction between communication and data management systems and security, which because of them exchange of commercial information in relation to the sale products or services, will be available, lead us to take into serious consideration some main components of electronic commerce and in particular, to consider communication systems, data management systems and security.

(Daniel B. Britton & Stephen McGonegal, 2007)

The term Business Model rose to prominence in the 1990s with the advent of Information Technology-centered businesses. The term is closely related to the emergence and diffusion of commercial activities on the Internet.

According to the definition of a business model by Weil & Vitale a business model is:

*A description of the roles and relationships among a firm's consumers, customers, allies and suppliers that identifies the major flows of product, information, and money, and the major benefits to participants (Weill & Vitale, 2001).*

A great deal of research has been directed towards classifying business models and grouping them into specific categories. The taxonomy frameworks of Business Models that are presented in the literature differentiate based on two factors:

a) Criteria posed for classifying Business Models, b) Objects classified, whether they are entire business initiatives (such as eBay, Amazon etc.), possibly combining various business models (Timmers, 1998; Rappa, 2001), or atomic business models that can be incorporated into an e-business initiative (Weill & Vitale, 2001).

Electronic Commerce (Business-to-Business, Business-to-Customer and Customer-toCustomer) is now growing at a spectacular rate. The people in business have to understand what is Electronic Commerce and what it is doing to their business, industry and society. There is a shift of power from the supplier to the customer and businesses must be consumer-centric (Turban, King, Lee,Liang and Turban (n.d.)). Information, not capital, is the keypoint of dot com (.com) businesses. Change is not constant; it is accelerating. Competition is constantly emerging from unforeseen areas. This has caused growing demand for Electronic Commerce education in all areas of business and information technology, management, finance etc. (Hromadka, 2000). As business needs are growing, more courses and programs that provide education in Electronic Commerce are needed (Mangan, 1999). Demand for Electronic Commerce education is high and growing.

(Milton Jenkins, 2001)

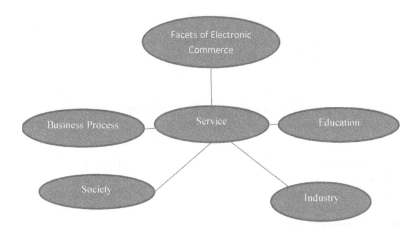

## 4.1 Classification of Electronic Commerce into specific categories

A common classification of Electronic Commerce is by the type of transactions and the relationship among transacting members. The major categories of Electronic Commerce transactions are (Turban, King, Lee,Liang and Turban (n.d.)):

- Business-to-Business (B2B): Electronic Commerce refers to transactions among organizations. Nowadays, about 85% of Electronic Commerce volume is B2B.
- Business-to-Consumer (B2C): Electronic Commerce includes retail transactions of products or services from businesses to individual shoppers. The typical shopper at Amazon.com is of this type.
- Consumer -to- Business (C2B): In Consumer -to- Business (C2B), people use the Internet to sell products or services to organizations and individuals. Priceline.com is a famous organizer of C2B travel service transactions.
- Consumer-to-Consumer (C2C): In this category consumers sell to or buy from other consumers. EBay sales and auctions are mostly C2C.
- Business-to-Employees (B2E): This category refers to the delivery of information , services or products from organizations to their employees. A major category of employees is "mobile employees" such as field representatives. Electronic Commerce support to these employees is also called business-to-mobile employees (B2ME).
- E-Government Electronic Commerce: In E-Government Electronic Commerce, a government agency provides products, services or information from or to businesses (Government agency-to-Business (G2B)) or from to

individual citizens (Government agency-to- citizens(G2C)). Also governments can deal with other governments (G2G)).

## 4.2 Electronic Commerce in Greece

Greece currently presents low levels of electronic commerce adoption but has the potential to grow fast. Although electronic commerce has been emerged as a global phenomenon and referred as the Global Electronic Commerce (GEC), several countries lag behind in terms of Internet services and electronic commerce use. Greece is the only member of the European Union that belongs geographically to South-Eastern Europe. The stability pact, for example, is an initiative made by the European Union and adopted in Cologne on the 10th of June 1999 (SCSP, 1999) in order to: "achieve the objective of lasting peace, prosperity and stability for South Eastern Europe".

Greece plays an important role in the region as an EU member state with political and economical stability and it can act as an exemplar for good practice (Rogers, 1995 p. 166) in terms of technological improvement and better use of electronic commerce.

The statistics about Internet and electronic commerce adoption in Greece are not very positive but they show steady and rapid growth. Specifically, according to European Union there were 7 Internet users per 100 inhabitants by the end of 1999 (EU average: 19), which shows an increase of 55% since the end of 1998 (EU average: 51%). Additionally, 32% of all companies had Internet access by the end of 1999 (EU average: 63%), which shows an increase of 28% since the end of 1998 (EU average: 27%).

The importance in the exploitation of information technology for the economic growth of the country has been recognized by the Greek government. According to the policy document "Greece in the information society" (The Greek government, 1999) the strategy for the Information Society in Greece was based on certain basic principles: • Innovation and entrepreneurship. The Information Society will develop based on market rules and mechanisms, and the institutional and regulatory framework should facilitate the development of new entrepreneurship and the creation of a culture of innovation. • Democracy and freedom. The Information Society should strengthen democratic processes and safeguard the rights of citizens. • Equal opportunities and solidarity. The Information Society should enable all citizens to have access to the knowledge and the opportunities opened up by electronic commerce use and should show solidarity towards those who fail to follow with new technologies soon.

**4.3 What may be the future of e-business in Greece?**

In recent years, electronic transcations through virtual stores in greek market are continuously growing. The rapid development of Information Technology-centered firms has positively affected the development of e-business in Greece.

**4.4 Some last conclusions about Electronic Commerce**

Since 1996, when the application of an electronic commerce policy started in Greece, there are some specific results in terms of Internet and electronic commerce use, while the prospects for future adoption and use seem to be even more optimistic.

- Electronic commerce helps communications and strengthens co-operation. To promote cooperation, it is important for policy makers to strengthen a fruitful coordination of the public and the private sector.
- Application of standards and cooperation at an international level is very important for a successful electronic commerce policy.
- It is important for policy makers at the highest level to take into consideration ideas and thoughts of stakeholders at lower levels of decision making. The knowledge of the market and companies needs can be very useful for designing an effective electronic commerce policy.
- The early electronic commerce experience in U.S. and Western Europe can benefit countries that are now at an initial stage of electronic commerce adoption.

**4.5 Connecting Digital Revolution with E-Commerce**

With the development of e-business focusing to business-to-business transactions, we are not just interested in measuring the impact of Information Technology on the productivity of organizations, but we are interested in seeing significant improvements in productivity by streamlining information and by improvements due to the decline of the cost of trade between organizations that make electronic transactions and apply the basic principles underlying the e-commerce.

We also have a particular interest in the use of Information Technology, in particular the applications of Information Technology and Electronic Commerce, in order to measure basic elements of the share capital. Share capital consists of all funds raised by a company in exchange for shares of either common or preferred shares of stock. The amount of share capital or equity financing a company has can change over time. A company that wishes to raise more equity can obtain authorization to issue and sell additional shares, thereby increasing its share capital (Kenton).

In our effort to understand the significant effect of eCommerce, we should compare:

- Business-to-business and consumer-to-business types of eCommerce.
- Digital and non-digital products and services. Non-digital products should be delivered to consumers with their physical presence in the store. Digital products can overpass the wholesale and retail practice of traditional trade.

The technological dynamics of the digital age continue to impact the decisions of firms.

According to what *Lenard and Britton say:*

*"The digital economy is creating an economic revolution, which according to the Emerging Digital Economy II (U.S. Department of Commerce, 1999), was evidenced by unprecedented economic performance and the longest period of uninterrupted economic expansion in U.S. history (1991-2000), combined with low inflation. Due to the growth of the Internet and its usage, hardware advances (PCs, cell phones), progress in communications capabilities (e.g., VoIP, worldwide broadband adoption), advanced usage of digital media (e.g., Internet video, blogs and wikis), and IT spending for better productivity, the future of the digital economy is looking good." (Lenard and Britton, 2006)*

| Field | Description |
|---|---|
| *Globalization* | *Global communication and cooperation* |
| *Digital System* | *All analog systems are converted into digital systems.* |
| *Markets* | *New competitive markets over the Internet* |
| *Businesses* | *e-business* |
| *Digitization* | *Digitization of books, music and other products and quick distribution of goods* |
| *New Business Models and Procedures* | *New Business Models and Procedures that offer new opportunities to businesses.* |
| *Protection from Electronic Frauds* | *Cybersecurity offers protection against malicious software and electronic frauds* |

(Turban, King, Lee,Liang and Turban (n.d.))

## 5. Digital Gap – A big challenge for the Digital Economy

*According to what George Mitakidis says:*

*"New technologies can bridle digital gaps. The rapid development of the digital era, which will bring positive changes and developments globally at both economic and social level, still presents serious risks that are centered on the creation of the digital gap. Among the different digital gaps, the most serious is mainly between the developed countries and the developing countries." (Metakides)*

## 6. Conclusions

The Digital Economy refers to an economy that is based on digital technologies, including digital communication networks and other related information technologies. The Digital Economy is sometimes called the *New Economy* or *the Internet Economy*. In this new economy, digital networking and communication infrastructures provide a digital global platform over which people and organizations interact, communicate, search information and collaborate. The technological dynamics of the digital age continue to impact the decisions of firms. If we consider in more detail a balanced view of the Digital Economy, we can tell that a balanced view of the Digital Economy perspective illustrates where technological dynamics are emerging and where more traditional patterns seem to be holding. Moreover, we have to examine the policy implications of the rising Digital Economy. The digital economy is creating a unique business culture and establishing a network of economic values critical to the next phase of change in our technological society. In the end, we must pay attention to some central topics such as new ways of organizing, the importance of vision and trust in e-commerce.

# Bibliography and References

Beat F. Schmid (2000): The Concept of Media in Lee, R., et al. (eds.) : Proceedings of the Fourth Symposium on Electronic Markets: Negotiation and Settlement in Electronic Markets, Maastricht (NL), Erasmus Universiteit Rotterdam, Euridis Conference, 1997.

Bloomenthal Andrew. What is Electronic Commerce? Retrieved from https://www.investopedia.com/terms/e/ecommerce.asp

Bohme Rainer (2010). Security Metrics and Security Investment Models. International Computer Science Institute, Berkeley, California, USA.

Business Week (2005). Retrieved on September 2010 from https://www.bloomberg.com/businessweek

Bo Carlsson (2004): The Digital Economy: what is new and what is not?

SCSP (Special Co-ordinator of the Stability Pact for South Eastern Europe) (1999). "Stability Pact for South Eastern Europe" Constitutional document Cologne, 10 June 1999 (www.stabilitypact.org)

"cnet.com". Retrieved from https://www.cnet.com/news/google-finds-9500-new-malicious-web-sites-a-day/

Daniel B. Britton & Stephen McGonegal, 2007: The Digital Economy Fact Book from the Progress and Freedom Foundation

"Decision Support Tools: Porter's Value Chain". Cambridge University: Institute for Manufacturing (IfM). Archived from the original. Retrieved on 2010.

"Defining Malware". *technet.microsoft.com.* Retrieved from https://docs.microsoft.com/en-us/previous-versions/tn-archive/dd632948(v=technet.10)

Don Tapscott. The Digital Economy: Promise and Peril in the Age of Networked Intelligence .

Don Tapscott (1996). The Digital Economy.

Douglas, E. Comer (2007): Computer Networks and Internets with Internet Applications

Drucker, P. Managing in the Next Society. New York: Truman Talley Books, 2002

EBusiness Forum (2010). Retrieved on September 2010 from http://www.ebusinessform.gr

Financial Times (2005). Retrieved on September 2010 from http:// https://www.ft.com/

Georganta Zoe and David Warner Hewitt (2004), Information Economy and Educational Opportunities: A Latent Variable Model of Learning Skills.

Hromadka, Erik, E-Curriculum? How Are Indiana Business Schools Teaching E-Business?, "Indiana Business Magazine," February 2000 (44-2) pp. 55-61.

Heger Attaya (2009). Software piracy and producers developers' strategies. CEPN University of Paris 13 Juin 2009-06-24

Lenard, T.M., and D.B. Britton. "The Digital Economy Factbook," 8th ed. The Progress and Freedom Foundation, 2006. pff.org/issues-pubs/books/fact-book_2006.pdf

Mangan, Katherine S., Business Students Flock to Courses on Electronic Commerce, Information Technology Section "Chronicle of Higher Education," April 30, 1999. Page A25.

Metakides George, president of the Research Group of the European Council and member of the ESPRIT (European Strategic Programme of Research in Information Technology) Management Committee and of the NATO Science Committee at different times between 1984 and 1987

Milton Jenkins, A. (2001). Meeting The Need For E-Commerce And E-Business Education: Creatinga Global Electronic Commerce Concentration In The Masters Of Business Administration (MBA) Program. 1081-1086.

Mikko Hypponen (2006). Malware goes mobile. Scientific American Vol. 295, No. 5 (NOVEMBER 2006), pp. 70-77

Nirvikar Singh (2003): The Digital Economy

Heinz, U. (1986). Heinz responds. Physical Review Letters, 56(1), 94-94. doi: 10.1103/physrevlett.56.94

Kostner, J. (1996). Virtual Leadership. Secrets from the Round Table for the Multi-Site Manager, New York: Warner Books, Inc.

Mallas, D. (2010). Article from Imerisia Newspaper.

Papazafeiropoulou, Anastasia & Pouloudi, Nancy & Doukidis, Georgios. (2002). Electronic Commerce Policy Making in Greece.

Porter, Michael E. (1985). Competitive Advantage: Creating and Sustaining Superior Performance. New York: Simon and Schuster. Retrieved on April 2010

"Protect Your Computer from Malware". OnGuardOnline.gov. Retrieved on September 2010 from https://www.consumer.ftc.gov/media/video-0056-protect-your-computer-malware.

Rappa, M., Business Models on the Web, 2001, available at http://ecommerce.ncsu.edu/models/models_text.html.

Rogers, E. M. (1995). Diffusion of innovations, Free Press, New York.

Saranow Schultz Jennifer. The Rising Cost of Identity Theft for Consumers Retrieved on from https://bucks.blogs.nytimes.com/2011/02/09/the-rising-cost-of-identity-theft-for-consumers/

Sarianidis, Nikolaos and Kliani Afrodite (2008). The New Economy in Greece.

Seekingalpha (2007). Retrieved on April 2010 from https://seekingalpha.com/article/91597-take-advantage-of-phishing-scams-with-security-software

Schmid, Beat; Schmid-isler, Salome; Stanoevska-Slabeva, Katarina & Lechner, Ulrike: Structuring and Systemizing Knowledge - Realizing the Encyclopedia concept as a Knowledge Medium.1999. - Information Resources Management Association International Conference (IRMA 1999) "Information Technology in Libraries". - Hershey, Pennsylvania, USA.

TechTarget's IT encyclopedia. Retrieved from https://www.techtarget.com

Telecom Regulatory Authority of India (TRAI). Retrieved on April 2010 from https://main.trai.gov.in/release-publication/reports/telecom-subscriptions-reports

The Greek Government (1999). "Greece in the information society. Strategy and actions" Athens, February 1999 (http://www.primeminister.gr)

The Global Information Technology Report 2009–2010 ICT for Sustainability. INSEAD, The Business School for the World & World Economic Forum.

Timmers, P., Electronic Commerce: Strategies and Models for Business-to-Business Trading. Wiley, 1999

Turban, E., King, D., Lee, J., Liang, D. and Turban, D. (n.d.). Electronic Commerce.

William Kenton. Retrieved from the website https://www.investopedia.com/terms/s/sharecapital.asp

Weill, P., Vitale, M.R., Place to Space: Migrating to eBusiness Models, Harvard Business School Press, Boston, 2001.

# YOUR KNOWLEDGE HAS VALUE

- We will publish your bachelor's and
  master's thesis, essays and papers

- Your own eBook and book -
  sold worldwide in all relevant shops

- Earn money with each sale

Upload your text at www.GRIN.com
and publish for free